Sticky and Dangerous Plants

Written by Lee Wang

Flying Start
to Literacy®

Contents

Introduction

Some plants are dangerous to animals.

Some plants have seeds that stick
to animals. Some plants have sticky
leaves that can trap animals.

Some plants have
oils and saps
that are poisonous.

All these plants are
dangerous to animals.

5

Sticky seeds

Grasses

Some grasses have sticky seeds.

These sticky seeds have tiny hooks that stick to anything that comes into contact with them.

These seeds can stick to an animal's feathers or fur.

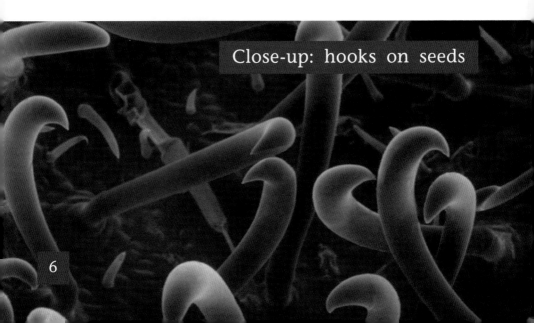

Close-up: hooks on seeds

If a bird gets lots of sticky seeds on its wings, the wings become too heavy to move and the bird cannot fly. The bird cannot look for food.

Burdock plant

A plant called a burdock grows
on farms and along fences,
roads and creeks.

The plant has prickly seeds called burrs.

Burrs have sticky hooks and loops that
stick to clothing and to animals' fur.

Burrs can get stuck in an animal's fur and make its skin itchy. This can be very painful for the animal.

Small animals such as bats and birds can get stuck to a burdock plant and cannot get away.

Plant traps

Sundew plant

The leaves of the sundew plant are covered with tiny drops of sticky liquid that look like water.

Insects drink the drops of sticky liquid.
They get stuck in the sticky liquid
and are trapped.

Then the sundew plant uses the insect
for food.

Pitcher plants

Pitcher plants have leaves
shaped like tubes. These
leaves can trap insects for food.

This pitcher plant has a long hollow tube with liquid in the bottom. Insects crawl into this tube, fall to the bottom, and drown in the liquid. The plant uses the insect for food.

Pitcher plants with teeth

This pitcher plant has tube-shaped leaves with slippery edges. When an insect lands on a leaf, it slips and falls inside the leaf.

When the insect tries to get out, it gets trapped by the sharp teeth on the leaves. The plant uses the insect for food.

Poisonous plants

Cactus tree

The sap of this cactus tree
is dangerous to animals.

Animals become very sick when
they eat the sap. When the sap
gets on an animal's skin, it can
make the animal itchy and give
it blisters. An animal can go
blind if the sap gets into
its eyes.

Hemlock plant

The leaves and roots of the hemlock plant are poisonous. If cows and horses eat this plant, they can become very sick and they can die.

Foxglove plant

The flowers of the foxglove plant
are poisonous.   Animals can become sick
if they eat the flowers.

Conclusion

Some plants are dangerous to animals.

Animals can get stuck in sticky liquids.

They can get sticky oils and saps on their skin. These itch and burn.

Animals can get sick and they can even die if they eat these plants.

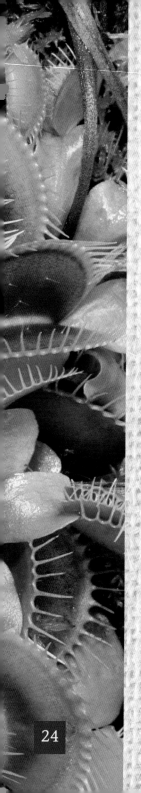

Glossary

blister: a small watery sore on the skin

burr: a prickly seed

liquid: something that is runny

oil: slippery liquid that is much thicker than water

sap: liquid found in some plants

tube: something that is long and hollow